Words That Matter

*

Poetry

Gerry Sikazwe

Mwanaka Media and Publishing Pvt Ltd,
Chitungwiza Zimbabwe

*

Creativity, Wisdom and Beauty

Publisher:
Mmap
Mwanaka Media and Publishing Pvt Ltd
24 Svosve Road, Zengeza 1
Chitungwiza Zimbabwe
mwanaka@yahoo.com
https://mwanakamediaandpublishing.weebly.com

Distributed in and outside N. America by African Books Collective
orders@africanbookscollective.com
www.africanbookscollective.com

ISBN: 978-1-77906-354-0
EAN: 9781779063540

DISCLAIMER

All views expressed in this publication are those of the author and do not
necessarily reflect the views of *Mmap*.

Acknowledgements

The author would like to thank Abigail Shachinda of A.rts, New Ink Review, Tendai Mwanaka, Gankhanani Moffat Moyo, Bhekumusa Moyo, Kafula Mwila, Marita Banda, Norman Shoe Sitali, Mirriam Chitambo, Emily Chendauka, Mutinta Numbwa, Geoffrey Mutale, Simon Mbayoni, Elijah Nonde, Mable Chanda, Angelina Shamuzumba, Mark Chingumbe, Dale P. Wimbrow, Global Platform Zambia, and specially his parents Fredrick Kasonso Sikazwe and Mpande Clementina Chisukulu Sikazwe, and every person who informed the making of this project. Above all God, for providing the aforementioned.

Dedication

To this generation, and those to come.
LUSWEPO

Table of Contents

Songs & Hearts VII

Introduction

What is poetry? Poetry is an epitome of words that matter to both the audience and the poet. Poetry has the deepest connection between man and reality while it also remains both a reality and a reflection of reality.

A lot of people have understood poetry to be a written art form. However, through *Words that Matter*, Gerry has deliberately chosen to place the word whether spoken, imagined, assumed, or written at the centre of poetry. Poetry cannot be restricted to the written form because not only does it predate writing, it is linked to the origins of language. When students of language argue, through the Singsong theory that language started through song as a way of reducing on the weight of labour, one notices that they place poetry at the centre of language because at the centre of the song is poetry. While the student of music will focus on melody and other aspects of music in the song, the student of poetry focuses on the words, the lyrics. This therefore means that the song at the centre of the origin of language is the poem. It is for this reason that poetry should be seen more central to language than any other art form.

Many Eurocentric writers have thought poetry to be an art form primarily written. I wish to argue that in African and many other traditional societies, poetry has existed for times incomprehensible in oral form. What does this say about poetry? It basically shows that poetry has no special inclination to writing; it is meant to be shared through any medium that uses language as a communication path. I therefore find Gerry's title, *Words that Matter,* a comprehensive title for this work. The collection is a collection of words; words that matter to man and to the art form. Gerry has such a rare gift with words that his poetry feels fresh whenever one encounters it whether in written or oral form. This freshness draws the reader back to the word every now and again.

It is my wish to present to the reader this work that in my perspective is a good representation of our poetry, our words, our art, our being.

Gankhanani Moffat Moyo
Poet & Author, Orgasm
Lecturer, University Of Zambia.

20 October 2018
LUSAKA

Dares & Dreams

birth reveries
grand and boundless
realities majestic

GLOW

Who will you be tonight?
Will you be the moon,
Or the fresh wind that accompanies it?
Will you be the brightest star,
Or the darkness that peeps behind it?
Who will you be tonight?
Will you be that dancer everybody prays they tango with
Or will you be that one who ignores the luring call of music on to the
floor?
Will you be her, the one with a warmly burning smile,
Or him coldly quiet, afraid to loosen his laughter?
Who will you be tonight?
Do not be me,
Do not be them,
Just simply be you, and glow.

In Your Hands

You hold wet clay,
In your palms shapes forming,
Skins smoothing and curves widening,
Molding tomorrow into a beauty unique,
A future with charming bewitchment.
You hold a pencil,
On white paper to run,
Pressing and printing; drawing,
Mounting your obese dreams,
So life may have purpose.
You hold a feather,
With which your mind to speak,
Echoing your thoughts, loudly singing,
Writing of days afar where fear is toothless,
Where winds are wings, with which unrestrictedly you fly.
You hold stars,
In yours palms, and violently they burn,
Desiring to brighten existence,
Design them so then into galaxies, awe striking,
For hope, to always twinkle at earth.

There Is More

There is more
    do not be afraid
stick out your hand and grab
    do not be afraid
hold out your hand and catch
    There is more out here
There is more
    do not shy away
boldly walk on to glory
    do not shy away
fearlessly sail on to nirvana
    There is more out there
There is more
    do not wane
O human eye dare to see more
    do not wane
O human feet care to walk more
    There is more out there!

I Hear Cries At Night

I hear cries at night
Not of little birds whose nests
cold has besieged
Not of wandering dogs sleepless
and hungry
I hear cries at night
Not of tires tired screeching
on Tar roads
Not of foolish chatter or breaking
of bottles at pubs
I hear of cries at night
And these are cries of dreams undreamt
Loud wails of possibilities willfully ignored!
I hear cries at night
And these are cries of hope given up on
Screams of faith forsaken and utterly despised!
Every night I hear cries
Every night I hear these cries
And just wish you too could
So that we can hush them together!

From Now On

From now on
    We will not wait for another
To advance our causes
     But ourselves as one
From now own we'll act
From now on
    We will not sleep till tomorrow
To speak and chant
     To sweat and create
The sanity we've been desiring
    From now on we'll act
From now on
    We will not wait for anyone
To plant or harvest our fruits
    We are enough a people
To swing hoes and sickles
    And so from now on we'll act as one
For ourselves

I Will Not Be Broken

I will not be broken
I will not be broken
down to dust
I will not be shaken
I will not be shaken
down to naught
I am going to be
What mother
birthed me to be
I am going to grow
Into a reality father
Dreamt I will become
I will not be broken
I will not be broken
down to dust
I will not be shaken
I will not be shaken
down to naught
I will not run away
But stand and bloom!

Our Identity

Our identity is not what they think we are
We are only what the soil that holds our umbilical cords says we are
- sons of the soil
- daughters of the land
Our identity is not what they hope we are
We are only what palms of fathers' love and mothers' hearts
gravened us to be
- creations of love
- love, itself, alive and whole
 Our identity is not what they expect us to be
 We are only what winds and clear skies beckon us be
- birds free and beautiful
- stars giant and bewitching
This and only this is our identity!

Onward, Forward

(for Mr. Andrew Ntewewe, YALI ZM President)

"Where do we go to
from here?"
screams the voice of a protester's
nubile nudity
"Where do we go to
from here?"
rants the diverse tongues of blood
of our forefathers and mothers
"Where do we go to
from here?"
questions lips of Ghandi proudly
"Where do we go to
from here? "
echoes the dream of a civil rights' fighter
"Where do we go to
from here?"
sharply orates beyond color and race
the prisoner president
"Where do we to
from here?"
sings words of the phenomenal songbird
of old
"Where do we go to
from here?"
whispers the lips of this time
we are in

And now that we are here
"Where do we go to
from here?"
I too ponder!

These are cries of hearts crushed by pain,
They are words of voices slain!

These are whispers of stitched voices unheard,
They are sketched signs of crippled wishes unread!

O Poet!

O poet bleed your pen
Our pains to forecast
----will you!
Rest not your hand
Even when its voice grows hoarse
Speak forth our troubles
Our losses and fears
Weave us hope with words
----your pulse sings
O poet speak our case
For beastly hearts of men and time
to hear
To hear you
And finally listen to us, to our cries!

I'm A Girl, So Was My Mother!

(for daughters and mothers)

They smoke our brains black,
Until to ash, then dust, they kick us
Into graves of oblivion, societies of non-existence
Us burying
Us forgetting
Us throwing in the back
Locked in the bedroom
Rocked on beds into submission
They smoke our brains black,
Until to ash, then dust, they kick us
Into graves
With germinating fruit in our wombs
Our girls,
Other girls,
To be second-placed,
Ever unacknowledged
Never to be counted

Just like our mothers
Just like ourselves
Our daughters are prey!

What Of Us?

Grace is for believers,
Dreams are for those with beds,
Light is only a gift to those with sight,
And time a slave to those who can tell it.
But what of us,
Who cannot tell time because (at us) the Sun no longer shines,
Who lack sanity of the eyes, with visions impaired,
Who know no beds, and no sleep,
Us whom grace cannot save since we do not know what to believe?
What of us,
Us, for whom the cold of nights was created,
Us whose stomachs hunger is daily bread,
Us whose hearts are too numb to wish,
Us, presently, suffocating in clenched fists of ignorance and poverty?
But what of us?
What of us really?

Never Settle: Claim Back All

For anything less than your worth
Everything slightly like or more like
Or even "like-like" is not to be settled for
In fact never settle,
Want more, ask for more, take more until you have it all,
They have stolen much from you
Than their speeches sketch or ever will
Than their acts of goodwill repentantly claim
And much more from them you must recoup
Never settle for anything they throw at you,
Small compensations or insincere apologies
Those are sweets they make you lick
At the expense of your tummies' eternal emptiness
Those are banjo-stringed tunes they play to sooth your ears with
While still chaining your minds and hips from dancing enjoyably
Never settle for anything they easily hand you
For anything that is easily handed off
Is valued less by the hand that gives it away
Yours is to demand and take pricelessness,
Anything and everything short of such, spit on!

Vultures & Hyenas

They use us for their fattening
Sell us soothing tales
In exchange for their lavish lifestyles
They eat what is ours
But close doors into their homes
While we starve on roads leading to their residences
They are vultures and hyenas
After our insides and bones
But will not allow us taste their meat!

Music Still Speaks

Music on lips of babies
still speaks
Realities adult minds willingly
ignore
Chaos and animosity fresh
and frequent
Music on lips of babies
still speaks
Shameful misfortunes daily!
Hearken to the resounding cries
from sore childly throats
Realities adult minds willingly
ignore
They speak of now, now whose madness
we overlook perpetuating!

Future We Want

How lovely is the thought
of the future we want
Built with finest steel and gold
Adorned in finest wool and glass
How lovely is the thought
of the future we want!
But see, this future
will not be handed to us
For this future cannot be handed to us
It does not exist
We must create it
Mold it with palms of our minds
Build it with the hands of our sweat
The future we want does not exist
The future we want cannot exist on its own
It must be created
And only we can create it
Only we must create it
For only we know it!

You Are Freedom

From the four ends of the earth,
Soft sounds of comforting words are sailing,
Whispers of an assured fate are heard,
That one day man shall be free, even from his own chains.
Mouths are loudly singing this tale,
Trumpets do echo this tiding,
Pencils are sketching this portrait,
And feathers do pen this dream.
But do you want to be free, to think with your own mind?
Do you want to see me free, whistling my own tune?
Do you really want this for us, freedom?
For our freedom to ashes burns,
Right in our insanity of chaotic philosophies.

Patriotism

patriotism is not
anthem singing mate—
sweat for lyrics' aim

Blessed Curses

Let them choke
On their curses
Let their insults
of you
Leave them toothless
Let them perish
poisoned from meals
they've served you
Let them never awake
from graves dug
for your bodies
as ghosts or gods
Let them never be
Evermore
If ever they attempt
to hurt
or hunt
or haunt you!
Let them never see light again
These godforsaken oppressors!

Soothes & Clouds

black thick lips smiling
glistening river of joy-
tar road leading home

Oases: Our Women

You cuddle our dreams
With abundant love
Wrapped securely inside infinite
Assuring hugs and nudging pats
You tirelessly serve us

But often your sweat dries up unwiped
But often you are rewarded thanklessness

You water us with hope
Our roots to never thirst
Our leaves to always sparkle
Our lives to ever sublime into
Realities only dreamt of

But often your sweat dries up unwiped
But often you are rewarded thanklessness

You offer yourselves selflessly
Feeding us your whole
Like stars killing your dreams
To nurse and fatten our own
Like rain draining yourselves
To water our being into flowers beautiful

But often your sweat dries up unwiped

But often you are rewarded thanklessness

If You Can, Do

Someone somewhere needs a prayer,
    If you can, do pray for them,
Someone somewhere needs a miracle,
    If you can, do give them.
Someone somewhere wishes,
    If you can, command the stars to grant them,
Someone somewhere dreams,
    If you can, paint their much yearned reality.
Someone somewhere craves warmth wool fails to give,
    If you can, do hug them,
Someone somewhere yearns belonging,
    If you can, do take them in.
There is a lot of bad around,
    If you can do any good, do,
There are many faces tear stained,
    If you can write smiles on them, please do.

Out There

Watching you hurt
and afraid
pains me enormously
Seeing you try
and fail
weakens me badly

I pray you find
Closure

One day.

We Are Not Afraid Of The Dark

We are not afraid of the dark
    We are the dark
For in it our beauty shines bright
    And our being glorified
We are not afraid of the dark
    We are the dark
For in it our brokenness is strength
    And our being is unashamed
We are not afraid of the dark
    For in it we are made whole
In the depth of every night's blackness
    In the belly of lightlessness
We are not afraid of the dark
    For in it we are made perfect
In the cold arms of harshest times
    Inside the embraces lacking warmth
We are not afraid of the dark
    We are the dark
In its purest form and entirety.

Worn Boldly And Gratefully

But as life has day and night
Mine too has faces
One of glittering smiles
And another of darkening frowns
One impressively witty
And another shamefully imbecilic
But as life has day and night
And is proud of its fraternal twins
I too am not embarrassed of mine
I wear them boldly and gratefully
Knowing
That if not for them
The balance they shape
I would be a life mad and dangerous!

When I Break

When I break
I do not hide my brokenness
I denude my broken parts
out of the closet of self-pity instead
When I break
I do not hold back my tears
I let them run down
flow madly as if fountains
Because when I break
I shade of parts that are imperfect
And arise as a phoenix
from flames of flaws and ashes of shame
To glory glittering
So when I break
I break openly and heal just as so
Openly!

Once At Night

Once at night
Poor men become kings
And in their darling royal dreams
Over the universe they supremely rule
When in day they are but only servants.

Once at night
Life becomes so surreal
Very simple and without order
Women and men as one sleep
Children and gods as mates play
To echo just how compatible all is.

Daily Prayer

Today is a prayer answered
-A miracle in flesh
And in its fullness we shelter

Tomorrow is a prayer rendered
-A dream anticipated
And in it too we shall flourish!

Inside Our Hearts

There is a place for rest
A place with enough room
Ten of our worlds would fit
and more
There is a place of comfort
A place serene and bright
Where everything there
Is a moon or a star
Shining
In the core of our hearts
Where love as a stormy sea
rages madly
Where Eden still flourishes
ever green

Only,
In that place of rest in our hearts

Light
(for Luswepo E. Nakazwe)

Inside your eyes
little sister
sits father's
pointing us to a future
glorious
for us he dreamt
Keep them open
and let them burn
lighting our paths eternally
faithfully walking us through life
as he would himself!

One Day We Will Come Back Home

One day we will return home
Not today
        Not tonight
Not even tomorrow maybe
        But soon enough
But one day
        Surely some day
We will come back home
        Where we belong
In your arms father
        On your laps mother!

Depths & Deeps

I cannot remember it
               Nor forget it…

My Nebuchadnezzar's dream!

There

We will get there
Somewhere
Anywhere
Eventually!

I Must Eat The World

I must eat the world
Eat the seven layers of the world
its flesh
Adding form to my stature
And sparkle to my skin's shine.
Travelling the earth;
I am to meet faces and
Lips
Shake hands and
hug thighs
break bones and
cry a little
sing poems
and dance to life
exploring world's in others' minds
Sailing out onto the open seas trapped
inside other's eyes
To view what lies beyond my sight
Tasting what beauty exists out there!
I must eat the world
Travelling it wide and through.

I must eat the world
And I hope to do so with you!

A Backpack of Bones and Hair

I carry my past on my back
Asleep and dreaming
I carry love lost in my pockets
Forgotten and wishful
I carry shame on my head
embarrassed and weak
I carry hopelessness on my forehead
desperate and broken
I carry bones of dead dreams in my eyes
distorted and haunted
I carry restless souls of undone deeds inside my mind
stubborn and mumbling
I carry death deadly in my heart
mindless and blood-thirsty
I carry doom inside cells of my body
unforgiving and uncaring!

I own this backpack of bones
and hairs
Yet still I choose to walk on
Yet still I choose to hope on
For I know tomorrow will soon be here
And then I will shine!

What Folly Is?

What is folly?
Licking dry armpits of life
Seeking your thirst to quench!
What is folly?
Following visions of blind seers
To lead you to glory!
What is folly?
Feeding on the young
Expecting a fattened tomorrow!
What is folly?
Despising guidance from graves
Hoping to welcome grey hair!

But Not Anymore

I've drunk vomit drooling from
fermented-folly filled mouths;
Talks of irredeemable imbecility.
I've licked puss rotten oozing
from spanked bums of the silly
Lipstick stinky unfit to be kissed!
I've fellowshipped in cursed shrines
where insults and vanity are incense
Companies of useless profane idiots.
But not anymore
But not any more

I found purpose, and a name
To perform, and protect!

Tears Of Beds

We all can see and feel
agony served in broad day light
We all can recognize tears
from eyes of a child
Yet how many of us
can sense silent agony in the night
can tell apart tears and the rain
For when its dark and quiet
Is when fears torment loudly
Is when tears fall profusely
Wetting beds, beds which ought
to be for comfort
Scaring dreams, dreams of fleshy nirvanas,
with despair
Yes how many of us
can see and feel agony served in the night
can recognize tears from eyes of grown men?

I Miss You

Whenever I look deep
into your eyes
I see you are still in there.
Whenever I listen acutely
to your voice
I hear you are still in there.
I just hope you are happy
and it is
worth it being out there.

Truth & Lies

"...These words, these words I drum
Shall beat on and on teaching wisdom
Even when my cobra skinned drum
forgets its tune, and no longer beats..."

We Owe All To Them

(for Mr. F.K Sikazwe & Mrs. C.M.C. Sikazwe)

We fly on wings
Strong and swift
Of those that breathed
Before our births
We thrive on ideas
Dreams and creations
Of they that conceived us
First in their minds
And finally in their wombs
We owe all to them
We owe them our being

In Solidarity

Today together we spoke
in different signs and symbols
One message
Today together we stood
On fresh feet, wooden legs and steel wheels
For one cause
Today as one we sung
proudly
claiming what belongs to us
our birthrights
and desires of our hearts
And, in solidarity, as such we won!

Not All

Not all flowers deserve to be picked
Not all stars twinkle to bless the night
Not all pearls must be sought.

Good Men Do Good

"To expect bad men not to do wrong is madness!"_ Marcus Aurelius

To expect good men
not to do good is unthinkable
Good men do right
Just as bad do wrong
To expect bad men
not to do wrong is folly
For bad men do bad
Just as good ones do better
But again to think neither
Is capable of either
Is being blindly hopeful
And lamentably devoid of reality!

How Is The Future Safe?

How safe is tomorrow
in the hands
Of those who die tonight?
How bright is the future
inside eyes
Of those who, to lust of gold, have lost sight?
How outspoken is eternity
on lips
Of those whose mouths drool greed and lies?
How possible is tomorrow
if painted by
boiled brains and drunk fingers of youths?

Hope

The lie of hope is
That in the end all ends in perfect bloom!
The truth of hope is
That in the end all ends in perfect bloom!
And this is the absurdity of life!

Wisdom, Heed It

What elders speak in a shout or whisper,
Heed.
What elders echo in pen or thumb,
Heed.
What elders suggest in a sigh or a murmur,
Heed.
What elders rant in a nod or a wrinkled face,
Heed.

Turn Lies Into Truths

Let us turn these lies
into truths
We have kept them
but they do us no good
Let us turn these forgotten pasts
into cherished memories
We have neglected them
yet they are what we need to thrive
Let us turn these wrongs
into rights
So that maybe again
we can dance
in the belly of fire and not burn!

Risk It All

Risk it all
Put your heart out there
To finally laugh
a little
To finally live
a little
Risk it all
Put your heart out there
To finally love
a little
To finally have
a little

Risk it all
Put your heart out there
and live!

To Know Truly

To know who truly
Stands for you
You've got to fall
Hitting hard on rocks
You've got to lose
Fading your glitter
You've got to fail
Stitching shame to your name
You've got to lack
Desperately needing help
And then
You'll know who truly
Stands for you!

Live Today

Do you not
Know
tomorrow
we die?

Undressing Life

I have seen insanity and sanity
dance as one
before eyes of the undiscerning!

You Make The World What It Is

For you hold a brush in one hand,
And a bowl of color in another,
To make the world blue as skies,
To make the world green as fresh grass,
With beauty and life folded in peace.
For in your heart grows love,
And in your soul flows a stream of happiness,
To make the world lovelier,
To make the world happier,
With immortal warmth and unrestricted joy.
For your choices and decisions are pencils,
And your dreams and wishes are crayons,
Which sketch the world's morphology,
Which shade thickly the world's skin,
With precision as that of a star's twinkle.
You are a potter, molding the world,
With your thoughts and actions,
You are a sculptor, carving this world,
With your philosophies and actual deeds,
This world is as you've made it to be.

I Am Not My Own

I am not my own,
For I had nothing to do with my existence,
I was merely a thought mercifully conceived in the creator's mind.
I am not my own,
For I did not design nor decide what skin dark or bright to
permanently wear,
I was clothed in black earth following the potter's careful image.
I am not my own,
I am nature's because I swing on icy strings tied around its hands,
I am my land's as my existence is the extension of its love,
Not my own, never my own.

Suddenness Of Death

We die aboard buses to our futures.
Excited and expectant.
O how sudden the wind of death
Blows
uprooting and breaking
trees shooting for the stars!
We die aboard ships to our tomorrows.
Sad and surprised.

Life Happens To All

Peering into eyes of fire
I see anger
defiant like no other
burning
hatefully like lava inside bellies
of furious volcanoes
And the fact that every man
Or woman in their existence
will one day or plenty more days
endure the bites from this
ferocious beast
Become harshly certain
I am compelled to advise you
to brace yourselves therefore
for this fire burns even for you
only time will tell your turn
But I know it is soon!
- mine was yesternight -

Warring Beings

We are all at war
Fighting battles inside of us
Even if in others eyes
we stand as the very epitome of peace
Our worst fear
is to be seen for who we really are
make-up and costumes down
Bruised, cursed, enfeebled
Our greatest worry is
being known for what we really are
When stripped bare
of what glitter we wear
Troubled, despaired, dying
Warring brings!

Smiles Do Not Mean Smiles

Smiles
don't often mean so
  - cheerfulness
 - solace
 - hope
 - sunshine
 - roses
 - rainbows
Smiles
don't often mean so
Sometimes they just are masks
stubborn
Unwilling to be taken off!

Rare Things

Truth
on lips of teachers and preachers
Love
in hearts of lovers and friends
Wisdom
in deeds of the wise and old
Hope
in dreams of children and youths
Life
in blood and bones of the living
Reality
on palms and soles of time and existence!

Politics: Foul Song

A song
sung off-tune
often
than clinically
A melody
Tepid
tastelessly foul
danced to by all
unfortunately
the greedy rich smiling
As they enjoy the fat meat
at the high table
of national stakes!
And the poor hungry wailing
As they bury their youth
and old dying
from politics' blood thirsty Pangas!

Kitchen Knives Nowadays

Kitchen knives nowadays
wake up under pillows from beds
proud having been of service!

Kitchen knives nowadays
fancy not cutting Onions
but spousal jugulars
tears and screams summoning

Kitchen knives nowadays
thirst not for blood of tomatoes
but love to wine and dine on the
redness of lover's flesh

Kitchen knives nowadays
wake up under pillows from beds
mostly rusty unused and unhappy!

Lord Be With Me

Shine my every path
With hundred suns during day
Thousand moons at night
And millions of billions of staring stars always
Making sure that lost,
Alone far from you I never trail
But that in the palms of your hands
I play, work and die
But that in palms of your hands
I wrinkle and sleep into man heaven will welcome.

Songs & Hearts

Is love the smile of the morning sun,
Which gives us hope for the day?
Is love the stare of the moon,
Which assures us that the night will be okay?

I Will Listen, Do Tell

I can see it in your eyes, it reddens them,
I feel it in your voice, it chokes you,
I know something is vexing you, do tell.
Do tell please, I will listen.

Notice Me

Watching stars burn, twinkling
Inside the black of your eyes
Evokes in me desires enslaving;
Passions that tickle my heart,
Emotions that trigger thirst for you.
And now
Sore and sorrowful, my soul bleeds!

Temporary Forevers

Let me give you a piece
of skies
a feel of clouds
a taste of wind on your tongue
And the smell of paradise

Let me give you a piece
of night
a touch of stars
a sight of cosmic beauty
residing in my eyes

Let me give you a piece
of eternity
a dose of forever
a mint of tomorrow bright
here in my arms

Let me give you a piece
of skies
a feel of clouds
a taste of wind on your tongue
And the smell of paradise!

Complete Me

Make me sane
Clever and knowing
Make me strong
Harnessing fear and pain
Make me meek
cautious and caring
Make me saintly
giving and forgiving
Make me crazy
wild and free
Make me weak
scared to forfeit you
Make me proud
boastful of a jewel I have
Make me selfish
Ever wanting you for myself!
Complete me
Complete me

Love Your Smile

Love your smile
Beauty is not
what they say it is
Beauty is not
Skin color
Hair type
Curves or lack thereof
Tall or short
Fingers or nails
Lips or nose
Cheeks or dimples
Eyes or ears
Mini-skirts or robes
Beauty is none of those
It just is
It just is you
On any day
With your smile worn
partially or completely
With your smile printed
Proudly or shyly

Beauty you see
Just is
It's just you
On any day
With your smile worn

Playfully or seriously
Loudly or noiselessly
Love your smile
Beauty is not
What other's eyes say it is
It just is
You!

In Billions

A billion thoughts fill
my mind
Racing
Bringing joyful memories
sweet
Of your gay smiles
Dressed in finest Masai clothe
A billion dreams fill
my nights
Completely
Teeming with music
Pure
Of your words, sighs and laughs
Dipped in wild African honey!

All I think of is you...

Where Love Dwells

We found love
warm
in places
we sought it not
in forms
we thought it not
In cold arms
of lonely women
Inside chests
of heartless men
On tongues
of lying fools
Inside eyes
of nuns
In cries
of pets we own
In songs
of birds in the wild
On peaks
of giant mountains
In bellies
of abysmal seas

And as unlikely as this
We found it there
warm
And as unlikely as this

we found it fully blossomed

Fire & Ice

Worlds apart
-day and night
-flesh and stone
-fire and ice
In love strangely
And strongly so
Tell me
But why can't this be?

Good Goodbyes

I never was
I never am
Good at leaving
Or being left
I never was
I never am
Good at saying bye
Or being told so
That now I wonder
If there is anything good
in byes
Or if good goodbyes even
exist.

Do you really have to leave?